The Slip

by Michael Montlack

POETS WEAR PRADA • HOBOKEN, NJ

The Slip

First North American Publication 2009.

http://pwpbooks.blogspot.com

Grateful acknowledgment is made to the following publications where some of these poems have previously appeared or will soon appear:

Arts & Understanding, Black Robert Journal, Chiron Review, Columbia Poetry Review, Court Green, Danse Macabre, Ganymede, Gertrude, Mudfish, New York Quarterly, and *Velvet Mafia.*

ISBN 978-0-9841844-2-2

Printed in the U.S.A.

Cover Illustration: "In Your Old White Shirt," charcoal and oil on paper, 2003, Christopher Shields.

Author's Photo: Nicolas Arellano

slip

to become involved or absorbed easily.

to lose one's foothold.

to be said or revealed inadvertently.

to make a mistake or error.

to deteriorate.

to be lost.

to pass from the mind, memory, or consciousness.

to neglect or miss.

to get away or free oneself from.

"give somebody the slip"

to escape from someone who is with you, following you ...

You can sit outside his door and wait ...
[or] you can dedicate your pain
to him.

~ Stevie Nicks, "Thrown Down"

Contents

Acknowledgments

About the Author / About the Artist

Also by Michael Montlack

The Slip

Is it possible
to have been tattooed
by someone's soul?

    Only with eyes closed
    can I trace outlines,
    a slight raise on my unmarked skin
    (even in creases: inner elbows,
    between fingers and toes).
    The designs always familiar
    but too abstract to identify.

I mean, can one be widowed
by the living?

    Carting the blank stone
    from days into dreams
    toward an open grave
    in my front and back yards,
    basement, bathtub.
    Ever eluded by the body,
    not the scent.

And if there is someone else one day,
will he sense this presence?

    The fine slip beneath
    my rumpled clothes.
    The railing I reach for
    even on shallow stairs.

Will you
be the mosquito netting
draping my honeymoon bed,
swaying almost imperceptibly in the dark
but allowing in breezes
that comb the hairs on my arms,
legs, chest?

boy witch

for three Halloweens
your mother, beautiful enough
to halt your old man's remarks
with a simple eye roll,
would allow, even encourage it:
buying the green face paint,
sewing and then letting down
the hems each year herself—

had your plastic wand worked:
perhaps a daughter for your mother?
or a sister for you
instead of two brothers.
maybe a potion to keep you
from outgrowing them,
some spell to stop them
from expecting tackle football.

but at seven there was no more
fabric to let out—and maybe
too little charm left in her eyes.
what a miserable cowboy you made.
an Indian would have been excuse
to paint your face again.

but no, that year your mother
revealed just how little power
she held in the world, and you
realized how little protection
you could offer her, even with
that shiny new dime-store magnum
your father put into your hand.

Vanity Smurf

Well, of course he stared at himself all day.
Everyone looked exactly alike—we're talking
a whole new dimension of clone here. Although
he was still by far the best looking of the village,
with a complexion even bluer than Smurfette's—
no doubt the result of some secret moisturizing routine,
perhaps a potion lifted from Gargamel's spell book.
Hey, a smurf's gotta do what a smurf's gotta do.

And expecting to be contented by workaday projects?
Gathering berries, thatching roofs, setting traps for Azrael—
all that drudgery and for what? To maintain some
god-awful strip of one-level mushrooms, like row houses,
a real estate fiasco (of mushroom-cloud proportions)
even the presence of ten Vanities couldn't appreciate.

His role was not entirely selfish, though—he
did introduce some much needed glamour and irony
(however unrecognized) in that saccharin world
always under attack and on the verge of being trampled,
where there was only a trollish Papa to be worshipped
but no Daddies, where males in Peter Berlin hip-huggers
were too busy skipping to strut, and where if a man
sought to eat you, it meant in that night's meager stew.

Yeah, if this is what you faced day in and day out,
wouldn't you cling to the familiarity of your mirror, too?

Under His Skin

at 15, your martini-mouth mother: *I know you're a queer*
Just make sure no one else finds out

16, Tacoma Grandma takes you in
never asking why you've come

17, art scholarship—New York

now 32, tattoos
       dragon, phoenix, Japanese clouds: all airborne
wrapping you like a shawl
biceps, shoulders, back
—nothing a dress shirt couldn't cover
should you ever trade
canvas for corporate
though they disappear
with my surprise naked
hug from behind

more artful
than Chinese characters (Life, Pride, Peace)
to you—Beauty, Delicacy
on a Nordic frame you wish
less lumberjack, more ballet—
something that could be lifted
by Japanese winds

But permanence, you say
that's the real thing—they can't leave
then you say little more
slathering sunscreens
to help preserve that indigo shawl
as if even there—sand-speckled, sweating—in August Maui
you're warding off, like Grandma, a terrible chill
freezing fiery winged creatures in flesh
like howls
stifled in a jar

Christopher's Mother

Does not hang on to her beauty
as tightly as it hangs on to her.

As tightly as her husband hangs on to her.

China in the grubby hands
of a clumsy child.

Hours of decoupage. Better
than conversation with him.
Surface treatment either way.

In her sixties. Slender.
Psychedelic muumuu. Just for fun.
Though she was too cool
for psychedelics
back in the Sixties.

Only at home in rentals.

In neighborhoods
where they can't afford to buy.

Invites her sons to visit.
Far better hostess
than mother.

Until: *Thank God for Christopher!*
Let's face it: my straight boys?
Rather *dull. I mean,*
BRING ... A ... BOOK!

Then: *Did I just say that?*
Oh well ...
Potato salad?

Family recipe. Served
with more vodka tonics.

While her husband shows off
her latest project.
His grandparents' dining table.
Completely puka-shelled and shellacked
but for a mahogany leg or two.

Portrait of an Artist

Collector of fractured things,
you long to lick patinas,
mouth watering at the flaking
of paint or rust.

Darning-needle hot,
studio window dog-cracked,
you sketch a better version of me
with a slightly larger nose.

Having almost known that beautiful woman
who was almost loved by a surgeon
willing to carve away
all that was not taut,
you seem almost ready now
to recognize her as Mother.

Though she has slackened
unrecognizably
beyond your charcoal lines.

Have you inherited the scalpel hand
from a man who aimed
to be your step-father?
Or just your own father's fear
of not seeing what's not there?

Breaking for wine
in crumbling Mexican tumblers,
you explain why you prefer others
to shop for the groceries:

Freedom, you say,
is browsing through knick-knacks
too bruised for sticky price tags.

Has your background
become your signature?
The relief in desiring
what most deem
un-willworthy.

Devil in the Doorway

You saw it there
in the dim entrance hall of your own loft:
burnt slick snake-skinned,
like a lanky manic mannequin
(some messenger?) standing firm,
ready to crash the gate.

This was September 10.
You'd taken an out-of-state friend
shopping downtown (Century 21)
and swore this thing
must've followed you home.
You first told me
our second night together—
instead of the usual
getting-to-know-yous: exes and fantasies,
fetishes, family.

There it was. This devil
in my doorway ... snickering at me
behind my friend's turned back ...
It taunted, savoring smugly
the dirty prank
before its execution
like a king entering
a burgundy-draped balcony
above the lion's pit.

You couldn't have sex
for almost a year after.
And the third time we did
(once the story had been shared)
I couldn't settle or blend
as if in an awkward threesome
with some cold new gender
that, laughing at our nakedness,
still refused to let us go.

Worse Than Cassandra

"The curse of the artist,"

you said, "is the ability to envision
perfect beauty
in a blemished world
incapable of realizing it."

And the work of the artist?

"To try anyway."

Did you explain this
before or after the kiss?

The kiss of the artist:
inside your Bergdorf Christmas window
behind the mesh *In Progress* screen
that barely shielded us
from rush-hour shoppers.

We were progressing.
Two? Three weeks?
And already a work visit.

The crystal droplets
of the hot-air balloon chandeliers—
your leaning on a ladder
in paint-speckled overalls.
Cassandra herself
wouldn't have seen the blood
on those gold-and-sterling-leafed walls.

The glass bubble
squared, seamless, dustless:
agreeable mannequins
ever-accentuating each other
in postures merely suggesting
relation and motion.

Like that blonde standing solo
in sleek rowboat, collared
and wristed in chunky diamonds,
evening gown dry, stance undisturbed
by posterboard waves.

Fashionable refugee? Titanic survivor?
Whatever the catastrophe,
past or pending,
the mesh screen lifting
would only reveal the moment
or idea of elegance
even in chaos, uncharted seas.

The diorama excused from explanations.
Your design portraying an excerpt
floating—if only

we could have maintained
that pose: two men kissing
in Bergdorf's window—
bold, sexy
and oblivious
(like the bejeweled blonde)
        to the Midwestern tourists
in town for Thanksgiving
and seasonal magic.

Should we—or you—have known
the ugly world never
would have held or showcased
us at our unreal best?

But the work of the artist
was "to try anyway,"
despite the curse, to create
an image of perfection
worthy of the occasion
but not so difficult
to disassemble.

Brothers and Sisters

Your older brother was stoned
during his bean-bag teens.
But at least would admit—
some twenty-odd years later—
that he had run away to Hawaii,
leaving you to fend off
Tacoma bullies by yourself
as your younger brother watched
through playground chain-link,
thinking but never saying
how much you deserved it
for ruining his reputation,
with your black nail polish and swagger,
pink-staining the family name
stitched into his Varsity jacket.

My older sister couldn't run
any further than the length of our drive
in her platforms: bangled and baby-oiled
gladiator in the hedged den of our yard,
screaming over the Stones on her portable,
"Just try it, ya little fuckers!"
at boys on bikes who rode by looking for me
while my twin sister, barely beyond
doll houses, consulted me
with dog-eared Sears catalogs—
furniture and bedding crayon-circled
for her dream bachelorette pad
"fully equipped," she'd remind me,
with a spare bedroom decorated
with my particular taste in mind.

It's some time since we've ended, Chris.
But I still wish
I could've spared you somehow—
a sister. Could have given you
some of that female love   so
you might've been strong enough
to believe a man could love you.

The Oversized Corduroy Comforter

I bought
once I sensed you were going to leave
smells only like me. Sometimes like steam
when I sleep with it pressed against the radiator.
But mostly like me.

You often said my scent was stronger than yours.
Musky, you called it. *It gets me hard.*
(But my sister just says B.O.
whenever I crash on her sofa.)
You said everything about me was stronger.
That you hated how I'd likely move on
faster than you would.

My friend Paul's bed smells like pot
even when we haven't smoked.
Like his Medicinal-Marijuana-Activist boyfriend.
Especially at the end.

Paul and I have been sleeping together lately.
No strings. For company.
He calls himself a widow but says he knows he'll get by
when I hug him in the dark after we've come.

I'd feel foolish talking to him about you.
Because you're not dead. Or even sick.
Just gone.

Paul showers with lavender and lemon soaps
and burns Nag Champa nightly.
I think he's waiting for the pot smell to lift.
To know he's finally healed.

These days I like sleeping at his place.
Or at my sister's.
Because my bed just smells like me.
My 'musk.' Strong.
Reminding me that I'm not going anywhere.

The Mythology of Death

Hades, also known as Aides—
the "Unseen"—became invisible
when wearing his helmet, a gift
from the Cyclops.

Deaf to flattery, numb to sacrifice,
the underworld ruler was once moved
by the sad song of a beautiful and talented man
seeking his lost love.

Orpheus would later turn to men
after his wife died the second time.

Could even the god of darkness be that dark,
as to inflict the same grief twice, opening wider
the already infinitely gaping wound?
Greedy to sustain all his tenants,
his wealth of death, it seems yes.

Such power appears cowardly
armed with invisibility
against a weaker race
so dependent on sight,
(and to think—this gift,
for a god with everything,
had come from a creature
with just one eye.)

Do they—our lost lovers
and our lovers yet to be lost—
expect us to attempt similar
senseless journeys? To sing,
to beg, to offer our gifts
for yet one more chance
to lose them?

Helmet-less, we don
our only protection:
We already love men
and know how to turn to them
in the repetitious waves of grief.

Gertrude, you had Alice.
But I had him (so briefly) and now we don't even talk.

"Well, you could just call him.
You could just call. You could.
You could say something.
Something about anything.
About anything you might want
to call him about. About him
not calling. About wanting to call.
About wanting him to call.
About him calling you. You could
say anything or something.
Or even nothing. About you. Or
him. Or you just wanting
to call. Or you just wanting him.
Yes, you could call about something,
even nothing. Call about you
just wanting him to call. About you just
wanting nothing. Or wanting him.
Wanting him to just want something.
Want you. Or you to call. You could.
You could say anything at all about him.
About him not calling. About
wanting him to call. Or him wanting
something. Or nothing. Or wanting you
to call. Or wanting you. Or something.
Something of that nature. Or the nature
of something. Of calling. Or not calling.
Or wanting. Or not wanting. Or nature.
The nature of wanting. Or wanting him.
Wanting him to call. Or wanting to call him.
Wanting him to want to call. To say
something. Anything. Anything that might
want saying. Before nothing more
is not said. Before more nothing is said.
Because nothing is more nothing
than not saying something when
something wants saying.

And that, well that's something."

Faux Finish

You spray-painted gold
that cardboard pyramid
for my niece's ice skating routine:
the tri-fold—bottomless.
No one'll see from the bleachers:
another example of your audacity
to build without foundations.

How darling, mothers would say,
wanting to rent your talent,
fringe it with tassels or taffeta
to match Sarah's leotard, Lyndsey's tights.
Long Island mothers feel they've spent wisely
when they hire gay.

My niece tossed the pyramid
like a ten-year-old Cleopatra
when she heard you'd gone.

Done with props and themes,
she skates team synchro now
while I avoid sideline mothers
looking for my "artist in residence."

"Uh, didn't you get the memo?"

We're no longer doing your hair
or telling you what to wear,
arranging wildflower bouquets,
selecting colors for duvets,
treating your windows or your walls,
planning your galas and your balls.

We're like ... busy.

Making our own lives
uber-fabulous.

I mean, why sing for supper
when the food tastes like shit?
Entertain yourselves, folks.
We boys have had it.

We're through making your soirees
more glamorous—or less pathetic—
filling lulls with witty remarks,
offering 'unmatchable' aesthetics.

Michelangelo painted the chapel
that wouldn't marry him today.
But we're registering at Tiffany's,
arranging our own wildflower bouquets.

So take a course in Arts & Crafts,
buy a glue gun or sewing machine.
The support staff has been promoted!
Your court jester is now the Queen.

House Beautiful

The mild one mixes fluorescent martinis
while his boyfriend guides the tours,
luring pairs of linen-clad guests
through lacquered halls, glossy rooms
visited by editors and on the verge:
their own spread.

Every now and then, he offers
a pause
before annotating: custom stained-glass doors
on some dead Dame's armoire,
now deemed perfect for DVDs.
Or some aside on costs, fine-line laws
to avoid when shipping
from third worlds.

His gestures—animated and precise
as a game-show model's—
alarm Baby, their drowsy French Bull
awaiting chase from her curl
on the lounge's silk throw.

No one leans on the treated walls
or rests a cocktail spent—
the coasters themselves (Venetian?)
worth framing.

Even the 70's spare room,
potentially *passé* anywhere,
seems *period* there.
How groovy, someone says,
the notion of a spare room
in Manhattan!

Then before pressing on,
the host bends to scoop
their quietly sauntering Baby,
collecting her in the cradle
of his long, gathering arms.

The Yellow Bathing Suit

I pick it up, wring it out (wonder when
my niece started wearing bikinis)
then hang it out with towels to dry.
No doubt I saved her from a scolding.

My sister scolds even me: *You're 36.*
You're throwing your money away renting.
I tell her I'll buy. When I meet someone.
Yes, everything ... when you meet someone.

Oh, Uncle Mike ... Uncle Mike?
I'm asked to abandon my book and the a.c.
for another game of Marco Polo.
I know with her parents making dinner,
she and the neighbor girls need supervision.
Or maybe she just wants to include me.

Once again, naval deep in warm water,
I am repeatedly calling out a man's name
and reaching for those slippery children
as they bob (*There! No, there!*) faintly
on a periphery.

Interior Design (Boys, Boys, Boys)

The Basement: Peter
foundation—early twenties
no longer dark or scary
a finished playroom: post-adolescent
glimpse of privacy

Roof-Top Viewing Deck: Roger
a telescope to locate him
though he rooted—there
behind me, preoccupied
with Venus or the wind chimes

The Bathroom: Two Quick Flushes
Scott at the vanity, clipping
snipping: *You're **not**
going to wear **that**?*
Or Eddie leaning over the toilet
hairy ass lifted, hairy toes jutting platforms:
Dunk my head, ya fucken bitch!

The Kitchen: Tyrone
chatting chitty chat chat
eating my mother's matzah balls
watching games with Dad
different team indifference

Master Bedroom: Chris
hugging sucking pipe-dreaming
less hugging, more sucking
jealous of Tyrone's kitchen,
a more-public *vertical* space

The Hallway: David
the long, narrow passage
that could've ended
in any room but ... no-
where to sit and talk

The Family Room and Vegetable Garden: _____
mortgage: meaning   to get them
finally done
with summer shares
and rent slavery

The Break Up

But still, how scary it is—to find love
now when we have only ourselves
to blame for annihilating it.

We could have, Chris.
We could have.

Or maybe we could have been lucky enough
to celebrate Stonewall—only briefly—
before watching each other waste away
faster than civilized countries
could give our disease a name.

We could have been carted away to camps.
Patched in pink then forced to bucket feces
on the lowest ring of Germany's *inferno*.

Once upon a time, we could have had little more
than occasional hours in rented rooms
as dark and vacant as our beard marriages.
Been trialed and sentenced like Oscar.
Or expected to condemn him
in polite dinner-party conversation.

Warren and Billy: Three Years into Fort Lauderdale

Warren's extended hand: *See, they do nice manicures ...*
over there at the strip mall, where Billy buys chlorine
for the paisley-shaped pool seldom used—an unbroken blue
like the hurricane-free sky: *Don't let it fool ya.*
Even their feisty terrier has carved herself a nest
between their sleeping legs since they left New York.
And oh, some of these palms will never be the same:
Billy, so mannerly, in muddied khakis and clogs,
preacher's son, goatee whiter against black skin.
He introduces me to his flowers, even those dying.
The most spectacularly potted—housewarming gifts.
Always more and more guys moving in round here,
Warren says, *who knows, maybe in twenty years, Michael?*
And oh, Billy says, *such a marvelous school district too.*

Acknowledgments

Many thanks to the editors of the following publications where the following poems previously appeared:

Arts & Understanding	"The Mythology of Death"
Black Robert Journal	"Interior Design"
Chiron Review	"Worse Than Cassandra"
Columbia Poetry Review	"The Yellow Bathing Suit"
Court Green	"Devil in the Doorway"
Danse Macabre	"Portrait of an Artist" "Warren and Billy"
Ganymede	"Faux Finish" "The Slip"
Gertrude	"Vanity Smurf"
Mudfish	"Under His Skin"
New York Quarterly	"Uh, didn't you get the memo?"
Velvet Mafia	"House Beautiful" "The Oversized Corduroy Comforter"

"The Break Up" received Honorable Mention for the 2009 Gival Press Oscar Wilde Award.

Michael would like to express his deep gratitude to Christopher Shields for sharing his beautiful artwork. It is an honor to have it on the cover and a joy to collaborate with such a kind friend. Thank you again and again.

(By the way, Christopher Shields is **not** the *Christopher*/artist mentioned in the poems of this chapbook.)

About the Author

Michael Montlack is the editor of the essay anthology *My Diva: 65 Gay Men on the Women Who Inspire Them* (University of Wisconsin Press, 2009) and the author of two other poetry chapbooks: *Cover Charge* (Winner of the 2007 Gertrude Prize) and *Girls, Girls, Girls* (Pudding House, 2008). His work has appeared in *Cimarron Review, Swink, New York Quarterly, Poet Lore, Court Green, Columbia Poetry Review, MiPOesias* and other journals. Recently he was awarded residencies from Ucross (Wyoming), Soul Mountain Retreat (Connecticut), VCCA (Virginia) and Lambda Literary Retreat (California). He splits his time between New York City (where he teaches at Berkeley College) and San Francisco, and has just finished writing his first novel.

About the Artist

Christopher Shields' work draws upon personal experience to portray aspects of modern gay identity. An MFA graduate of Minneapolis College of Art & Design, his work has been shown nationwide and can be seen on the web at http://impactfolios.com/christophershields. He lives and works in Chicago.

Also by Michael Montlack

My Diva: 65 Gay Men on the Women Who Inspire Them
(University of Wisconsin Press, 2009), Editor

Girls, Girls, Girls (Pudding House, 2008)

Cover Charge (Gertrude Press, 2007), Winner of 2007
Gertrude Chapbook Competition for Poetry

www.ingramcontent.com/pod-product-compliance
Lightning Source LLC
Chambersburg PA
CBHW061759040426
42447CB00011B/2385